MW01493975

NOVENA
to ST. JOSEPH

By

Rev. Daniel M. Quackenbush, OFM Conv.

Illustrated

C.B.   P.C.

CATHOLIC BOOK PUBLISHING CORP.
New Jersey

NIHIL OBSTAT: Rev. Msgr. James M. Cafone, M.A., S.T.D.
Censor Librorum

IMPRIMATUR: ✝ Most Rev. John J. Myers J.C.D., D.D..
Archbishop of Newark

Dedication

For Daniel Joseph Willett
and for all children who grow up in homes
without their fathers,
that through the intercession of
the great St. Joseph,
they may be protected and provided for
and, especially,
that they may know the Heavenly Father
and His infinite love for them.

(T-19)

ISBN 978-0-89942-193-3

© 2006 by Catholic Book Publishing Corp., N.J.

Printed in China

catholicbookpublishing.com

21 LP 2

FIRST DAY

St. Joseph, Patron of Families

ST. Joseph, the Church throughout the world honors you as the *Patron of Families*. Surely divine providence led you to embrace Mary as your wife. When she was found to be with child and you intended to "divorce her quietly," the Lord sent His Angel to intervene and led you anew to accept Mary as your spouse: "Do not be afraid to take Mary your wife into your home . . . it is through the Holy Spirit that this child has been conceived in her" (Mt 1:20).

Joseph, your marriage was part of God's plan, indeed, and as husband of Mary you were immersed in the great redemptive mystery of the Incarnation. What a trustworthy soul you must be, called as you were to be husband and father in the home that sheltered God's Son and His Immaculate Mother Mary!

Before the awesome responsibilities you faced, it would have been easy to lack courage. But Almighty God does not assign a role in life without providing the necessary graces. You had experienced God's guidance and protection and you knew that He was with you. You trusted in His love for your family and with confidence you followed His lead—protecting them from a pagan and hostile world and working at your carpenter trade daily and generously to provide food, clothing, and shelter for your family. You likewise served as educator to Jesus, teaching Him about life, about carpentry, and about the Jewish Faith.

You were a kind and just man, Joseph, but you were human and subject to fall—not divine like the Child you protected, nor sinless like the Virgin you guarded. In the home of the Holy Family, your heart was the most vulnerable opening for sin to enter. Yet you faithfully cooperated with divine grace by living a life worthy of the innocence and purity of your charges! You cultivated within your home a spirit of prayer and devotion! Had not the Incarnate Word of God Himself come to dwell in your home as your Son, still your home would have been one in which God's Word was welcome and lived.

St. Joseph, intercede for families—the sanctuaries of life. May couples discern God's will concerning their call to marriage and be confident in God's blessing in their homes. May they generously cooperate in His loving plan and be co-creators with Him in giving life. May families be protected from anger and hatred, lies and selfishness, infidelity and divorce.

Pray for us, Joseph, that children may honor parents and that spouses may honor one another. May children know patience and kindness and share these same virtues with their brothers and sisters. May single-parent homes and orphans be blessed with peace and security and the love and support they need to live happy and blessed lives.

St. Joseph, Patron of Families, pray that Jesus may be welcomed into our homes and be the center of our lives, as He was in the life of the Holy Family. Then our homes will be filled with God's love—they will be filled with God—as your home in Nazareth was. We ask you for these blessings and for all of the intentions we bring before you in this Novena *(pause).*

Rosary and Litany of St. Joseph (see p. 32)

Prayer

Let us pray: Lord Jesus, when You took on human flesh in the womb of Your Virgin Mother You identified with all humanity. Similarly, through the home You shared with Your Mother and St. Joseph You identified with all families. You know what a sanctuary a home can be for nurturing life and love. You are aware of the responsibilities that family life imposes upon us, as You submitted to the guidance of Your earthly parents and learned each day to contribute to the well-being of Your home.

We thank You for our families and for the love we share in them. Heed the prayers of our patron, St. Joseph, who so faithfully fulfilled his role as father and husband in Your home in Nazareth. May our families be protected from all those things that threaten our peace, harmony, and joy.

May Your love reign in our homes, as it did in Your home in Nazareth, and flow out beyond our walls into the neighborhoods and world in which Your Father has planted us as sources of grace and blessing for others. We ask this, Jesus, and all the intentions we bring before You in this Novena in honor of St. Joseph, the *Patron of Families.* ℞. Amen.

St. Joseph,
Husband of Mary

ST. Joseph, we come to you today under the title *Husband of Mary*. Almighty God had performed a special miracle by preserving your spouse from all sin from the first moment of her existence. Her Immaculate Conception was the miracle that anticipated the Incarnation. God would humbly become a human being, but He would take His humanity from a spotless Virgin.

If God was so careful in preparing a worthy mother for His Son, how careful He must have been in selecting for that mother a worthy husband. He who preserved her from sin surely would guide her to the man He had chosen to act as protector and provider for her home. Thus they would work together as trustworthy stewards of His loving plan of salvation. St. Joseph, you were that chosen one, called by God to become the Virgin's husband.

Among the Jewish people, parents and family members often arranged the marriages of young people while the couples themselves had little or no input regarding their partner. Nonetheless, Joseph, your marriage to Mary was surely a match made in heaven! This does not mean that your marriage was without your consent. God would not force Divine Motherhood on Mary. He certainly would not force upon her a marriage she did not want.

So Mary uttered another *"fiat"* ("Let it be"), Joseph, to God's plan for her. She said, "Yes, Joseph, I take you to be my husband"; and you echoed her *"fiat"*: "I take you, Mary, to be my wife." Then you took her into your home and the two became one. Your union was not sexual, but there can be no doubt that you shared an intimacy that reflected God's own love. If the foundation of the home is not its children but the love of husband and wife, how ineffable must have been your love, when the Child in your home was Love itself. How pure and life-giving must have been your love, when it was God Himself Who called you together.

We ask you Joseph, to pray for our world today. May young people be protected from the devious trend in our culture that regards conjugal relations superficially and attainable without commitment or sensitivity to the dignity of others. May Church pastors and ministers be more effective in "educating the ignorant" of our day with regard to the sanctity of marriage and conjugal relations. At a time when the very institution of marriage is debated, may we rediscover with awe and appreciation the design of the Creator in the structure of Nature and in our mutuality as male and female.

Many married couples experience serious problems today that threaten their mutual commitment. Pray for them that they may be given the grace of perseverance and faithfulness. Intercede for spouses that they may imitate Mary and you and dedicate themselves to accomplishing God's will together and bearing much fruit for His Kingdom. Pray for all marriages, Joseph, especially those we now mention in the silence of our hearts *(pause)*. We pray for them and all the other intentions we bring before you in this Novena.

Rosary and Litany of St. Joseph (see p. 32)

Prayer

Dear Lord Jesus Christ, we praise You for the wonder and beauty of marriage and family life. Today we contemplate the Divine Plan that brought Joseph and Your Mother Mary together as husband and wife. You experienced firsthand in your home in Nazareth the beauty of their love for each other and the security that such love brings. God's plan continues to bring men and women together in the sacred bond of marriage.

Yet, we live in a time when many marriages are in crisis and many children and adults suffer from the pain of separation and divorce. Even the institution of marriage itself is under attack. Hear the prayers we offer you on behalf of married life through the intercession of St. Joseph. Shed the light of Your grace on husbands and wives so that they may fulfill their marriage vows and love may reign in their homes and in the hearts of their children, as Love reigned in Your home in Nazareth. Grant young people the courage and selflessness necessary to respond to God's call to the Sacrament of Marriage and to commit themselves to its sacred bonds. Grant this most important blessing for our world, as well as all the blessings we ask for in this Novena in honor of St. Joseph, *Husband of Mary,* Your holy Mother. ℟. Amen.

St. Joseph, Patron of Workers

ST. Joseph, we honor you today under the title *Patron of Workers*. For your life's mission God gave you the astonishing responsibility of providing for His Only-Begotten Son and His holy Mother Mary. To fulfill this task you worked faithfully and diligently with your hands as a craftsman. Although you were never wealthy with regard to material things, you were able to provide your family—the Holy Family—with those things that they needed to live. Grateful for what you had and, indeed, grateful even for your ability to work, you offered your labors in a spirit of devotion and generosity to God, for the sake of Jesus and Mary.

Today there are many people who live in poverty and cannot find life-sustaining employment. Many leave their homelands in search of work to provide a better life for their families. You know what it is like, Joseph, to be a refugee, with your family in a foreign land. You are familiar with the obstacles that aliens encounter: prejudice, misunderstanding, injustice, exploitation, in addition to differences in language, culture, and religion.

Accompany these men and women on their journeys, often perilous as well as hopeful. Help them to find dignified work with just pay and a kind welcome. May they soon be reunited with their families.

St. Joseph, pray for all of us that we may always have fruitful and meaningful work. Intercede for the unemployed and for single parent families. Help us to know that as we make sacrifices to provide for ourselves and for our families we cooperate in the providential plan of our Heavenly Father and we reflect God's loving generosity to the world. Pray for us that we may work in harmony and mutual respect with our co-workers and supervisors.

In our pursuit of material advantages may we never abandon our faith, nor the priority of love of God and neighbor. Help retired people know that each day of life they receive from God's hand is a gift and that one never retires from the work of love. May we work together for the building of God's Kingdom in our workplace, in our families, in our hearts, and, indeed, throughout the world. St. Joseph, *Patron of Workers*, we ask for all of these things, as well as the other needs we bring before you in this Novena *(pause)*.

Rosary and Litany of St. Joseph (see p. 32)

Prayer

Lord Jesus Christ, You Yourself engaged in human work at home by faithfully fulfilling Your childhood chores and by assisting Joseph in his carpenter projects. Accept our daily efforts; bless them and make them fruitful. May every sacrifice we make be made for Your glory and for the benefit of our brothers and sisters.

Grant work to the unemployed and hope to those who struggle with financial problems. May they always turn in their need to the Father and provider of all. We ask this, Jesus, and all the intentions of this Novena in Your Name and through the intercession of St. Joseph, *Patron of Workers*. ℟. Amen.

FOURTH DAY

St. Joseph, Most Just

JOSEPH, today we honor you under the title *St. Joseph, Most Just.* This is the title with which God Himself first honored you when the Evangelist, inspired by the Holy Spirit, called you a "just man" (Mt 1:19). How much integrity must be yours for the God Who alone is just to have proclaimed you a "just man!"

You do not utter a word in Sacred Scripture, but this one word spoken of you speaks volumes. Like Noah[1] and Tobiah[2] before you, and according to the ideal to which the Old Testament called God's people for centuries, you embodied the virtue of God's own character by being a just and upright man.

You were "just," first of all, because of your devotion to God. You bowed to God's sovereignty and His right to intervene in your personal plans. When God claimed Mary, your betrothed, as His own and called her to be the Mother of His Only-Begotten Son, you responded in a spirit of service to His loving plan of redemption. You humbly obeyed the prescriptions of the Jewish law and offered to the God of Israel your faithful worship.

You knew, however, Joseph, that one could not be just toward God without also being just toward

[1] Gen 7:1

[2] Tob 9:6

11

one's neighbor. The Old Testament had long held up before the Israelite conscience the demands of justice, especially toward the widow, the orphan, the alien, the poor, and the oppressed. Surely you heard in the synagogue in Nazareth the indignant words of the prophet Isaiah directed toward people who attempted to keep their religion and relationship with God separate from a just treatment of neighbor:

> "This rather is the type of fast that I wish:
>   to loosen the fetters of injustice,
>   to undo the thongs of the yoke,
>   to set free those who are oppressed
>   and to break every yoke,
>   to share your bread with the hungry
>   and to offer shelter to the homeless poor,
>   to clothe the naked when you behold them
>   and not turn your back on your own kin."[3]

No doubt, your own life experiences also made you sensitive to the needs of those oppressed by cruel leaders and occupying armies, as well as to the plight of refugees and those who struggle to provide for their families by honest work in difficult times.

Religion—even your beloved Jewish religion—could be guilty of oppressing God's people, as well. Despite your devotion to the Jewish law, your just heart was not enslaved to it. When Mary was found to be with child, you put aside a legalistic interpretation of the Law and decided to divorce her quie-

---

[3] Is 58:6-7

tly, saving her from public condemnation and disgrace.

Instead of reacting with anger or revenge because of her apparent infidelity, you tempered strict Biblical justice with compassion. Although the Word made Flesh had not yet been revealed, you already had a sense that "mercy triumphs over justice."[4]

No wonder, then, that God chose you to act as the earthly father of that Divine Messenger of true Divine justice and mercy, His Son, our Lord Jesus Christ.

Intercede for us, St. Joseph, that we may bow before the majesty and sovereignty of God and allow Him to justify us—to make us just like you—in His Son. Pray that Divine grace and forgiveness, won for us by the great liberator Jesus Christ, may conquer sin, the oppressor of our souls and of all humanity.

In this day, Joseph, when the Church has proclaimed a "preferential option for the poor," help us to be sensitive to the needs of the poor everywhere and respond appropriately with fervor and generosity. May we have the courage and strength we need to confront the evils that oppress our brothers and sisters throughout the world today: homelessness, hunger, infanticide, abortion, war, violence, crime, racism, terrorism, economic inequity, etc.

Intercede for us, Joseph, that we may be just toward God and neighbor as you were, and dedi-

---

[4] Jas 2:13

cate ourselves as instruments of justice for others. We ask for these things and for all the intentions we bring before you in this Novena, *St. Joseph, Most Just (pause).*

Rosary and Litany of St. Joseph (see p. 32)

Prayer

Jesus, all-just, all-merciful Savior, we come to You once again in this Novena in honor of Your beloved servant Joseph. Today we appeal to him under the title that God gave him in Sacred Scripture: Joseph, the just man. May his prayers and example help us to accept the freedom You have won for us and strive to share that freedom with others. May we be sensitive to the needs of all of Your people, especially the most vulnerable and powerless.

Through the prayers of this humble servant of Your righteousness, may we become instruments of Your justice and mercy in our homes, our communities, and throughout the world. We pray for this and for all of the intentions we bring before You in this Novena in honor of Your devoted servant, *Joseph, Most Just.* ℟. Amen.

St. Joseph,
Most Chaste

JOSEPH, today we honor you under the title *St. Joseph, Most Chaste.* The children seers of Fátima said that the Blessed Virgin recommended you to us as a model of holiness. "If only the people of the world understood the holiness of Joseph, my spouse," she said, "they would know so much more about the road to God." What is the secret of your sanctity, Joseph?

Is it because you fell in love with Mary, a woman as "pure as the driven snow"? Is it because you treated her with great dignity and reverence, even before you knew that she was to become the Mother of God? Is it because you remained faithful to your commitment to marry her and faithful to your marriage vows even though Mary, the Mother of the Incarnate Word, was to remain Ever Virgin?

How selfless was your love for her and for Jesus! Although you were the "man of the house," you were not overbearing or demanding. Rather yours was a gentle and generous presence—a chaste presence— the holy presence of a just and kind man of God.

St. Joseph, at Fátima when your Immaculate spouse held up your sanctity as a model for us all, she also grieved that "more souls go to hell because of sins of the flesh than for any other reason." She likewise lamented the immodesty of clothing styles of that time. What must heaven think of the styles of today! Crucifixes hang on the walls of our children's bedrooms right next to posters of unclad men and women. Pornography has become multi-billion dollar annual commerce, oftentimes secretly invading our homes via the internet. Popular music videos and movies with alleged innocuous ratings leave little to the imagination and spew out sexual innuendo as regular fare. Our young people are sold the lie that sexual intimacy should be enjoyed apart from the sacred context of marriage and the co-creation of children.

Children are conceived and then, in the words of Olivia Gans, "slaughtered on the altar of sexual irresponsibility" by abortion. Even the Church, the Holy of Holies, has become a source of sexual scandal! It seems that the sin of lust has reached new heights of godlessness—a sin that can lead us to the unremitting horror of condemnation!

Intercede for us at this time when the virtue of purity is lost to us. Pray for us, that we may recognize the evil of lust in all of its manifestations and flee from it. Help our young people that they may look upon one another respectfully as brothers and sisters and mutually children of God. May they approach the wonder of conjugal love with reverence and gratitude, and trust in the wisdom of the Church with regard to sexuality and the exalted, sacramental nature of marriage and conjugal love.

Joseph, you were privileged to look upon God in the face of Jesus. Be our heavenly intercessor that we may be pure of heart and know and see God as you did. We ask you, *St. Joseph, Most Chaste,* to pray on our behalf for the rebirth of the virtue of chastity in our hearts and in our world and for all the other intentions of this Novena in your honor *(pause).*

Rosary and Litany of St. Joseph (see p. 32)

Prayer

Dear Lord Jesus Christ, we are a people of unclean minds and hearts, living among a people of unclean minds and hearts.[1] The culture into which You were born and lived was probably not much more wholesome than our own, although it is possible, that Your parents had more control over what You were exposed to than the parents of today. Nonetheless, Joseph protected You and Your Immaculate Mother from the evils of Your earthly days.

May his prayers protect us and our young people from the deluge of impurity and immorality that blinds our culture to the presence of God in our midst and in each other. May his intercession in behalf of the world help us regain the lost virtue of purity for ourselves, our families, and our society. ℟. Amen.

---

[1] Cf. Is 6:5.

St. Joseph, Protector of the Church

ST. Joseph, we come to you under your title *Protector of the Universal Church*. St. Paul tells us that, "When the fullness of time had come, God sent His Son, born of a woman, born under the Law, in order to redeem those who were under the Law, in order that we might receive adoption as sons" (Gal 4:4-5).

The Incarnation inaugurates the "fullness of time" of God's plan of salvation. The virginal conception of God's Son in the womb of Mary, your espoused, bridges heaven and earth, time and eternity, divinity and humanity. Such a critical moment in the history of our salvation and your personal, intimate participation in this saving mystery was part of God's plan!

Like Mary, you were visited by an Angel and asked to believe in the miracle of the Incarnation. Like her, you said your *"fiat"* ("Let it be") to God's plan of salvation for the world, and agreed to become the plan's humble servant, accepting the Virgin and the virginally conceived into your home and into your life. You thus became the guardian of this saving action of God, preserving and nurturing the Incarnate Word and His Mother throughout Mary's pregnancy, at the Child's birth in Bethlehem, and during the course of the delicate, vulnerable years of His infancy and childhood.

It is no wonder, then, that the Church turns to you as her protector and guardian. Not only did you faithfully watch over the Holy Family—model and type of the Church, domestic and universal; but also as spouse of Mary and foster father of Jesus, you were chosen by God to be the guardian of His saving plan for the world "in the fullness of time."

Protect the Church, which is the family of God, from the evils of our day, as you protected the Holy Family long ago from the clutches of evil. Intercede for us that the Word of God, which is Christ, may be preserved true and authentic and proclaimed effectively and courageously throughout the world.

Pray for Pope (N.), and for our Bishop (N.), and for all the bishops of the Church, called to be guardians and pastors of Jesus' flock. Through your loving guardianship, may the Church always be the sanctuary of Jesus' presence and the sacred place of encounter between the human spirit and the God Who loves and saves.

Through your prayers may the Church be preserved as Jesus' "spotless bride" and the "sacrament of salvation" for God's people throughout the world. St. Joseph, *Protector of the Universal Church,* hear our prayers for our holy Mother, the Church, and for the other needs that we bring before you in this Novena *(pause).*

Rosary and Litany of St. Joseph (see p. 32)

Prayer

Lord Jesus Christ, Bridegroom of the Church, You have built Your Church on rock and have promised that "the gates of the netherworld will not prevail against it." (Mt 16:18b). The "jaws of death" attempted to thwart God's saving action in the "fullness of time" of Your Incarnation by means of the depraved jealousy of the worldly king Herod. Joseph was the instrument that God used to protect You and, thus God's plan of salvation, from that evil threat.

The powers of evil continue to attempt to deprive the world of Your saving presence. May the powerful and loyal intercession of St. Joseph aid and foster the Church in our day in her mission of preaching Your Gospel and communicating Your Truth and divine grace to the world. We ask You for this grace, Lord Jesus, and for all the graces we ask for in this Novena in honor of Your humble servant, St. Joseph, *Protector of the Universal Church.* R/. Amen.

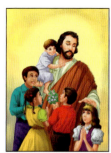

SEVENTH DAY

St. Joseph, Patron of the Unborn Child

ST. Joseph, we invoke you today under the title *Patron of the Unborn Child*. Just as God entrusted Mary with a critical role in the Incarnation of His Son, so too He called you to be intimately involved with this saving mystery. Mary lovingly carried God's Son in her womb for nine months and gave birth to Him. You were given the task of protecting and providing for Him, not only after His birth but also before He was born.

Your first reaction to this surprise pregnancy was to reject any responsibility for the Child. You had not planned on this Child, Joseph. He was not yours. You did not want Him—at least at first. So you decided to walk away from His Mother and from Him. But God had other plans for you and for your home in Nazareth. God had a plan for this Child. The Almighty had formed this Child in His Mother's womb; He knew His characteristics, talents, and potential. The All-knowing One knew this Child and He loved Him. It was God Who had sent Him to Mary and to you—and to us.

I wonder, Joseph, if you ever remembered your initial reaction to this gracious intruder into your life. Did you ever repent of your rash judgment of Mary and of your desire to "put her away quietly," along with the unborn Baby that she carried? Did you ever realize that if it had been your way, you would have missed having this Child as part of your home and your life? What a lost opportunity that would have been!

That is why you constitute such a fitting intercessor in behalf of the unborn. You know the importance of hearing God's will with respect to unborn human life. You know how people, refusing to accept an unwanted pregnancy, can dramatically and tragically go against the course of God's loving plans and lose untold blessings.

Tragically, alarmingly, abortion has become a way of life in our culture and in our time! Intercede for us, St. Joseph, that we may be enlightened to see the absolute value of human life. Intercede for those women and men who face unwanted, unplanned pregnancies. May they have courage and grace to accept responsibility for their unborn children and welcome them into their plans, homes, and hearts. Pray for medical personnel that they may recognize the violence of abortion procedures to child and mother and refuse to participate in them. Intercede for public officials that they may refuse to compromise the sacredness of human life for lesser values or political advantage.

Pray for us, that the Holy Spirit will raise up noble souls among doctors and nurses, government officials, church leaders, and all people of goodwill to courageously articulate the pro-life cause and defend life. St. Joseph, we ask you for these blessings and for all the things we bring before you during this Novena *(pause)*.

Rosary and Litany of St. Joseph (see p. 32)

Prayer

Lord Jesus, true God and true Man, Lord of Love and Lord of Life, hear our prayers and the prayers of Your servant Joseph on behalf of unborn human life. Your Incarnation manifests to the world of believers the profound value and potential of all human life. Forgive the outrageous ignorance and selfishness by which we so irresponsibly condemn unborn children to the slaughter of abortion. Grant pregnant couples courage and selflessness so that they may choose life for their babies.

May the conscience of our nation and of our world awaken to the supreme value of human life and the stark recognition of abortion as a "silent holocaust," which cries out to You for justice. Hear the prayers of Your servant Joseph, who experienced the human dynamics of an unplanned pregnancy, yet chose to care for Your Mother and for You through the grace of divine intervention. May the Heavenly Father's desire to give and create life not be frustrated by human selfishness.

We ask You to bless our world, Jesus, that the "culture of death" in which we live may become a "culture of life"—one that esteems, protects, and nurtures life. We ask You for these blessings and for all of the other intentions of this Novena, which we make in honor of your earthly protector and provider, St. Joseph, *Patron of the Unborn Child.* ℟. Amen.

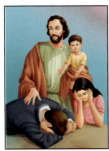

St. Joseph, Terror of Demons

ST. Joseph, today we come to you under the rather archaic title, *Terror of Demons*. The tendency to see demons "everywhere" has given way to a deeper understanding of physical and mental disease.[1] Nonetheless, the Gospel is replete with stories of souls afflicted by demons who found in Jesus liberation and healing.[2] Jesus Himself told the Pharisees that His expulsion of demons was a sign that the kingdom of God had come upon them.[3]

The many references to Satan and demons in Scripture, the Church's consistent teaching on the matter,[4] as well as many disturbing manifestations of evil in our day, all challenge us to soberly reflect on the presence of evil in the world and to seek divine assistance. Thus we come to you today, Joseph, for guidance and protection.

It is said in military circles that one must know one's enemy. Perhaps that is why you terrorize the devil and his army of fellow fallen angels, Joseph, because you understand well who the enemy is. "Arise, take the Child and His Mother, and flee to Egypt. Remain there until I tell you. Herod seeks

---

[1] See *Catechism of the Catholic Church* (CCC), #1673.

[2] See, e.g., Mt 8:28-32, Mk 3:11, Lk 4:33-36.

[3] See Mt 12:28.

[4] CCC, #s 398, 407, 409, 413, 414.

the Child to kill Him,"[5] the Angel of the Lord told you in a dream.

Your pure, virginal bride had conceived by the Spirit of God and given birth to Him Who would "save His people from their sins."[6] You had been intimately present to the miracle of that first Christmas night. But whereas the shepherds came in joy and wonder to see their newborn Savior, the corrupt king Herod searches for the Child to destroy Him.

The manifestation of evil in Herod's murderous scheme stood out in stark, shocking contrast to God's plan of "peace on earth" and "good news of great joy for all the people." You see very clearly the difference between light and darkness, love and hatred, good and evil. Temptation is subtle, but the majesty and beauty with which God showed himself to you in the faces of Jesus and His immaculate Mother made absolutely clear to your noble soul the vile, repulsive nature of evil. You thus definitively rejected its advances and lying seductions.

There is a war going on between good and evil, between God and His enemies,[7] Joseph, and at the time of the Incarnation you were placed in the heart of the battlefield. God relied upon you to protect His Son from the evil that sought to destroy Him before He could complete His saving mission on our behalf. You would resist the powers of hell wishing to devour the Christ Child, until His "hour" came,

[5] Mt 2:13.
[6] Mt 1:21.
[7] See Eph 6:12.

when He would lay down His life of His own free will.[8]

There are so many ways that evil shows its foul head in this our "culture of death"[9]: abortion, infanticide, genocide, war, terrorism, addictions, domestic violence, sexual exploitation of women and children, promiscuity, pornography—the list goes on and on! It seems that the devil and his demons are unleashed unchecked upon our world today. We turn to you, Joseph, soliciting your intercession in our fight against evil. You were so effective in protecting God's Son from the evil that sought to destroy Him before His confrontation of those destructive powers on Calvary. Now that you are allied with the victorious Christ in heaven, how effective must be your intercession to combat the evil that continues its onslaught against God's people.

Intercede for us, who are God's children through Baptism, that we may be able to recognize evil clearly and not allow its lies to entice us away from God's grace and love. Pray for those who are caught in the web of sinful habits. May we have the graces necessary to resist the demons that assault us each day: fear, despair, lust, greed, anger, hatred, arrogance, idolatry, and whatever other fiery darts the "prince of lies" hurls our way.

May the Church live and proclaim Jesus' victory over evil. Thus, empowered from above, may we be His instruments in confronting the powers of darkness that threaten the world's peace and salvation.

[8] See, e.g., Jn 10:18; 12:23.27ff.
[9] See *The Gospel of Life*, John Paul II.

We ask you for these things, Joseph, and all the petitions we bring before you in this Novena *(pause)*.

Rosary and Litany of St. Joseph (see p. 32)

Prayer

Dear Lord Jesus Christ, we thank You for the gift that St. Joseph is to your Church. We honor him today under the unlikely title for such a hidden, humble soul: *Terror of Demons.* Your earthly father serves as a wonderful sign to us that a life lived in simple faithfulness and devotion is pleasing to You and can be a powerful force for good in our world, assaulted by so much evil.

Joseph's quiet strength and effectiveness as guardian of Your Holy Family in the face of an evil that sought to destroy You, stands as testimony to the great divide that exists between heaven and hell and serves as a hopeful sign of Your definitive victory over evil, when You will kill the lawless one "with the breath of [Your] mouth."[10] May his example inspire us to seek what is good and holy and thus protect one another from the corrupting influence of the enemy of our salvation. Listen to his prayers on our behalf and drive Satan and his foul legion from our hearts and our world so that we may serve God and neighbor in peace and live forever in Your loving embrace. We ask You this, Jesus, and all the other intentions we bring before You in this Novena in honor of St. Joseph, the *Terror of Demons.* ℟. Amen.

---

[10] See 2 Thes 6:8.

St. Joseph, Patron of the Dying

ST. Joseph, for centuries the Church has had recourse to you under the title *Patron of the Dying*. What an honorific and significant title! "Precious in the eyes of the Lord is the death of His faithful ones," the Psalmist says (116:15). How trustworthy, then, must be your intercession on behalf of God's people at that crucial moment when our temporal lives end and eternity begins.

Various artists have attempted to put on canvas your own "precious" moment of death. With Jesus, your foster Son, and Mary, your spouse, depicted lovingly at your side—the Holy Family's grief appears before us with great mystery and drama. Death is something that cruelly invades the sanctuary of all families. Yet, no family ever confronted the starkness and horror of death with more clarity and aversion than did your family. No family ever experienced the grief of loss at the death of a loved one with the authentic emotion and pure love with which your foster son and your spouse faced your death.

If Jesus "was deeply moved in spirit and troubled . . . [and] began to weep" (Jn 11:33b.35a) when confronted with Lazarus' death, what must have been the sentiments of his heart at your death!

You were His foster father. You had provided for and protected Him. You had held Him in your arms and tenderly embraced Him. You had taught Him the Jewish Law and the carpentry trade. You had presided at His meal and Sabbath table. You were the loving husband of His blessed Mother. How deeply the experience of your death must have affected the Sacred Heart of the God-Man!

How clearly He must have perceived death as the enemy of love and of family. He Who would later say of Himself, "I am the Resurrection and the Life" (Jn 11:25), must have recalled the memory of your death as a rallying cry for His own battle with this great archenemy, when on Calvary He finally vanquished forever death's hold on the human family.

The other who held your hand at your deathbed, Joseph, was Mary your beloved spouse. As you looked into her sorrowful eyes, you looked into an ocean of compassion and sympathy. Yet, at the same time, you looked into the depths of an immaculate soul baffled by the harsh cruelty of death, which was stealing you away from her and her Son. You looked into an immaculate soul, which never should have been exposed to corrupting death—God's penalty for sin. As she sought to comfort you, she also expressed another faithful, but difficult *"fiat"* ("Let it be") to God's plan for her and her family.

As provider and protector, Joseph, you had sustained Mary and Jesus and shielded them from the world's harm. You could not preserve them from this moment, however, nor from the sorrows that would continue to confront them in this world after you were forced to leave them. You knew what it was like to be a father and husband and to fend for those placed in your care, but you were powerless now to assist them further.

Yet despite the intense human drama there was a love with an eternal character that reigned about your deathbed—a love that would ultimately laugh in the face of death, which presumed to break love's bonds. The force of that love had not fully blossomed, but it soon would. Then there would be a family reunion!

You had to have an inkling of this, Joseph, as you looked into the eyes of Jesus and Mary, as they so attentively escorted you to the door of eternity. You had been called to be father and husband by the Father and Eternal Spouse Himself. You must have known there would be another day.

St. Joseph, intercede for the dying and for their families. Help all those approaching death's dark and frightful door with your prayers. May they not despair but rather grasp the hand of the Savior and His Blessed Mother as you did. May their families lovingly accompany them at this "precious" time as Jesus and Mary accompanied you. May the love that they experience from families and other caregivers make their deathbeds a holy place, a place where love reigns and dissipates the darkness of death.

We ask you, St. Joseph, to intercede for all of our family members and friends who are dying, seriously ill or elderly, as well as for all the intentions we bring before you in this Novena *(pause)*.

Rosary and Litany of St. Joseph (see p. 32)

Prayer

Dear Lord Jesus, we thank You for the gift to Your Church of St. Joseph, *Patron of the Dying*. We ask You to hear Your foster father's prayers on behalf of all the dying and their families. You lovingly accompanied Joseph in his last moments and then ultimately freed him from death's bonds by Your own Passion, Death, and Resurrection. Through this great Saint's intercession grant courage and peace to all those who must confront the stark reality of death.

May they benefit from Joseph's great solicitude for them when that final moment comes and heed heaven's sweet invitation to an eternity of life and love in the family of God. We ask You for this incredible gift of eternal life for ourselves, our loved ones, and all Your people, as well as for the other graces we seek during this Novena in honor of your beloved servant, Joseph, *Patron of the Dying*. ℟. Amen.

APPENDIX

Litany of St. Joseph

LORD, have mercy.
Christ, have mercy.
Lord, have mercy.
Christ, hear us.
Christ, graciously hear us.
God, the Father of heaven, *have mercy on us.*
God the Son, Redeemer of the world, *have mercy on us.*
God the Holy Spirit, *have mercy on us.*
Holy Trinity, one God, *have mercy on us.*
Holy Mary, *pray for us.*
St. Joseph,*
Renowned offspring of David,
Light of Patriarchs,
Spouse of the Mother of God,
Chaste Guardian of the Virgin,
Foster Father of the Son of God,
Diligent Protector of Christ,
Head of the Holy Family,
Joseph most Just,
Joseph most Chaste,
Joseph most Prudent,
Joseph most Strong,
Joseph most Obedient,
Joseph most Faithful,
Mirror of Patience,
Lover of Poverty,
Model of Artisans,
Glory of Home Life,
Guardian of Virgins,
Pillar of Families,
Solace of the Wretched,
Hope of the Sick,
Patron of the Dying,
[Patron of the Unborn,]
Terror of Demons,
Protector of Holy Church,

Lamb of God, You take away the sins of the world; *spare us, O Lord!*
Lamb of God, You take away the sins of the world; *graciously hear us, O Lord!*
Lamb of God, You take away the sins of the world; *have mercy on us.*

℣. He has made him the lord of His household.
℟. And Prince over all His possessions.

Closing Prayer: (see prayer to Jesus at the end of each Day of the Novena, pp. 5, 8, 10, 14, 17, 20, 23, 27, 31).

---

* *Pray for us* is repeated after each invocation.